GW00360251

THE LITTLE BOOK OF
SLIMMING

First published in the United Kingdom in 2001

1 3 5 7 9 10 8 6 4 2

First published by Ebury Press
Random House, 20 Vauxhall Bridge Road, London SW1V 2SA

Random House Australia (Pty) Limited
20 Alfred Street, Milsons Point, Sydney, New South Wales 2061, Australia

Random House New Zealand Limited
18 Poland Road, Glenfield, Auckland 10, New Zealand

Random House South Africa (Pty) Limited
Endulini, 5a Jubilee Road, Parktown 2193, South Africa

Random House Group Limited Reg No. 954009

www.randomhouse.co.uk

A CIP catalogue record for this book is available from the British Library.

ISBN 009 188075 0

Editor: Mary Lambert

Designer: Jerry Goldie

Printed in Denmark by Nørhaven A/S, Viborg

THE LITTLE BOOK OF
SLIMMING

Margaret Miles-Bramwell

EBURY PRESS
LONDON

DEAR SLIMMING FRIENDS

For thirty two years, Slimming World has been offering slimmers the kind of support I know from personal experience is needed to take on the tough challenge of losing weight.

They have been incredibly happy and exhilarating years – and I have gleaned from even the sad, bad and mad times the wisdom that this little book shares with you today.

The millions of members who have walked through the doors of our thousands of classes throughout the UK have helped me to understand the process of changing weight as much as they tell me I have helped them. Changing eating habits is especially stressful. Making new healthy habits takes real effort.

There will be days when you need a small nugget of understanding from someone who has stood where you are standing and felt what you feel – and still does.

But losing weight feels fantastic!

You can do it! Take my word – and all of the words in this book – and go for it! And take with you my love and warmest wishes for your complete success.

Margaret Miles-Bramwell

You can break out of the
vicious circle of overeating,
being overweight, feeling
unhappiness, overeating – just
look for the help that is all
around you.

Don't just get help to stay
focused – give it where
you can.

Sharing ideas and thoughts
with friends about slimming
strengthens your own
motivation.

Moral support from good
friends when you're dieting
can bring you strength and
comfort.

Witnessing other people's
success at losing weight can
magically re-ignite your
impetus and bring your dream
back into focus.

Telling other slimmers how
you feel about your weight-
loss experience gives them a
feeling of hope when they are
beginning to despair.

Don't keep your worries
about your self image to
yourself – tell someone who
understands.

Slimmers the world over

befriend other slimmers.

Tell your friends you'd rather
have a good book than an
Easter egg.

Treat your friends to
a home-cooked meal.
Show them healthy cuisine can
also be filling and delicious.

Dine out, chill out,

be flexible.

Share in making someone's
dream reality – you'll share
their joy too.

Have a laugh every day –
it relieves stress and burns
calories.

Slimming is easier to do when
the sun shines, so make a new
summer resolution now.

Take the 'T' away from
can't and won't.
You'll find can and won.

The most powerful force working against your slimming success is often yourself.

The key to overcoming the
saboteur within is knowing
when it's at large.
Be aware – be very aware!

What has happened in the past

may have caused you to fail

but it doesn't define you

as a person.

It isn't a sin to be overweight.
It isn't a sin to be less than
perfect. It isn't a sin to eat
well and to enjoy life.

Tell your inner nagging voice
that says you're not doing well
to quieten down and give you
a break. Don't just turn the
volume down, switch it off.

Turn up the volume on your

inner nurturing voice.

Sometimes it's so quiet you

don't know it's there.

You don't need to beat
yourself up for having a bad
slimming day – you need a
hug. Give yourself a big one,
you need it.

Remember it's your inner
nurturing voice that has
wisdom and good taste –
your critical one has neither.

The one thing you need
more than a diet plan is
commitment, so don't start
without it.

Consciously, you know
you want to lose weight.
Subconsciously, you may
resent the need to change.

If you are finding this week
harder than others you aren't
a failure – it's normal.

And if you get back on your
weight-loss track next week,
you're above average.

Taking responsibility for your weight may mean coming out of your comfort zone. It takes courage, so don't underestimate it.

If our natural, healthy self
were allowed to emerge, that
self would be slim. Tell
yourself "I am slim. I am just
temporarily overweight-ing."

Repeated often, in the
present tense, "I am slim"
will charge up your belief in
your ability to be slim.

Understanding the past

helps us forgive ourselves.

The future is ours

to command.

Who do you want to be?

No answer – no goal.

No destination – no go.

Ask yourself – do I need to be
flexible with my diet today?
If you do, that's fine.

Focus on the next twenty-four
hours. That's as far ahead as
you need to plan for.

Picking up yet another rigid

quick-fix diet may be a trap.

Be afraid – be very afraid!

Do you always opt for boring
diets because you know you
will always give them up?

Have you ever considered that
it may be the diet that failed
you? If it required superhuman
effort, then you didn't fail,
it did.

Would you like to know
how to lose so well in just
one week that you'll be
hooked? Try your hardest to
prove Food Optimising
doesn't work.

I dare you to do it by the book – be relentless in your efforts to show that, while it may work for every other slimmer in the world, you are the exception that will prove Food Optimising is wrong.

You probably know most of
the ways to eat to lose weight,
but you may not know why
you don't use them.

Why bother to struggle with temptation? Take a five-minute break away from food.

You are not guilty of
overeating. Eating is not a
moral issue.

Do something that takes you
away from the sight of food.
If you still want to eat, make
sensible choices and enjoy
what you eat.

Be aware of what you are
eating – always be very aware.

Take a bite of your favourite
food. Taste it and really
savour its unique taste and
flavour.

Go slowly as you eat, and
think to yourself how much of
it do I really need?

Make decisions about what
you eat, rather than just eating
impulsively.

Use choice-power

not will-power.

Prepare before you shop.

Think of ways to avoid

impulse buying.

Shop with a list.

Impulse buying just puts
temptation in the food
cupboard.

Plan, plan, plan the food
you're going to eat, that way
you can relax.

Plan for lots of healthy food to

be freely available to you.

Plan for your personal trigger foods to be out of reach, and out of temptation.

Plan healthy snacks for those
times that you know catch you
out – when you first come
home from work, watching
TV, when you're feeling tired,
when you're bored.

Relax, relax, relax – planning
helps you to do this.

Have you congratulated
yourself today on how well
you're doing? What gets
praised, gets repeated.

Question your childhood
beliefs about food. Some may
have helped you gain weight.

Remember you can lose
weight at any stage of
adulthood.

Believe that you are in control

of your plan, because you are.

You may not feel in control.

That does not mean you are

out of control.

Do you think others know
better than you do about your
weight gain? Think again.

Do you think others know better than you do about your weight loss? Think again.

You know all you need to
know about the right weight
for you.

You are always sensationally
strong – especially when you
do not fret about
losing weight.

Your inner strength

is as great a resource as

any of your diet plans.

If a decision about a diet

is your own decision, it is

much easier to commit to it.

If it's not your decision,

you haven't made one.

You are the first person you
have to be honest with about
your eating.

Lies fatten —

truth flattens.

There isn't a diet lie

you've ever told

that I haven't told first.

Nice people tell white lies

and nice dieters tell

white diet lies too.

Diet lies are never deliberate

– they are just forgotten

foods.

Memory loss around food –

weight gain around hips.

Being overweight hurts
because others say it's
unacceptable, so this just
encourages you
to comfort eat.

Derogatory comments
about anyone's weight
are simply wrong.

There is no need to justify
yourself or your size – you are
not in the wrong.

One unhealthy snack doesn't

matter – repeated ones do.

Giving up your favourite foods

is a terrifying thought –

and extremely fattening.

Give your slimming plan an
extra stimulus. Write down
what you eat, as you eat it for
a few days. Keep this for your
eyes only.

Give up nothing. Enjoy
alcohol, high fat or high sugar
foods once in a while.

It's good for morale,

good for staying power,

good for losing weight and

good for keeping it off.

Be fascinated by your findings

about the way you eat. It is

the true way forward.

'Others eat like me

and stay slim.'

True – they do, occasionally.

'Others eat like me and stay slim.'
True – but this is because they're
more active.

Become active now – it's
possible to be fitter and still
overweight at the same time.
Become beautiful now – it's
possible to be attractive and
overweight at the same time.

You're more likely to keep
weight off in the long term if
you take some form of
exercise.

Begin to exercise, exercise
more often, exercise for
pleasure, exercise with
pleasure.

For success, always choose

a generous, flexible

eating plan.

Take full advantage of the food
you eat. Let it satisfy you and
nourish you.

Your body reacts exactly the
same whether it's the first or
the umpteenth time you've
started slimming. It's your
mind that's different.

Making up your mind that you will achieve weight loss is the foundation of success.

Create the most favourable
conditions in which to lose
weight, and you'll optimize
your chances of being slim.

Chew, chew, chew your food
well – it sends vital
information to your brain that
you are getting full.

Protein-rich foods such as
meat, fish and soya act as
superb appetite suppressants
for hours.

Complex carbohydrate foods
such as vegetables, potatoes,
pasta and grains do too.
Fats such as butter, oil, cream
and mayonnaise do not.

Fat has twice as many calories per gram as carbohydrate and protein. The same serving of fat gives you twice the number of calories as carbohydrate and protein with far, far less filling power.

Week after week, meal after
meal, most people eat the
same weight of food.
You can eat the same weight,
but you can vary its calorie
content dramatically.

Just the thought of not being
able to eat some foods makes
a diet impossible to stick to.
Be sure in your own mind that
there are no forbidden foods
in your plan.

Flexibility is the saviour
of many a struggling slimmer.
Dismiss any rigid diet rules
and embrace flexibility.

Give yourself a break.
The occasional lapse doesn't
ruin a healthy eating plan –
it just makes it easier to
live with.

Forget the word diet,
it really is a four-letter word.
Small, easy steps to regular
healthy eating will keep you
slim for life.

Think smaller in small steps –
a stone lighter, a size slimmer.

Always decide on your own
weight target, rather than an
ideal weight imposed by
someone else.

Picture yourself in your mind's
eye a size slimmer, trying
on some new clothes.

Picture yourself on the beach,

looking really good in a

skimpy bikini.

It doesn't matter if you're
never going to be thin – losing
ten per cent of your weight if
you are overweight will bring
you major health benefits.

Nothing changes

if nothing changes –

especially weight.

When you lose weight, you fall

in love with yourself.

Loving yourself is important to

your success.

Watch out for the triggers

that send your emotions

zooming downhill.

Stepping on the scales is
a hair-trigger situation.

No loss registered?

Despair.

A pound off?

Exhilaration.

Scales are a tool not a tyrant –
make friends with them.

If you do want to weigh,

once a week is the maximum

for inner peace.

Are you an angry slimmer?
Those who would like to help
you may back off.

Are you a defeated slimmer?
Those who would like to help
you may give up.

Have you ever been given

food instead of love?

How wonderful love tastes!

Have you ever been given a

sweet instead of a hug?

Hugs taste delicious.

Comfort eating has no impact
on your emotional needs and
too much impact on your
shape.

Overeating never satisfies

your emotional hunger.

You may not be able to
change anyone else's mind –
but you can change your own.

Emotional hunger will cry out

for satisfaction well before

your body needs more food.

See your emotional life as an
alternative to cooking not an
alternative type of cuisine.

It's OK to take time out of the
kitchen if your feelings have
taking a battering.

Has it occurred to you that
you are a wonderful and
beautiful person right now at
the weight you are? Forget
false modesty, you are superb.

When your confidence is low,
you may think only negative
thoughts. So write down some
compliments you've received
and read them regularly.

You're loveable – ask three
people who care for you to
tell you why.

Spend money on yourself now.

Don't wait until you've

become slim.

Wear a splash of bright colour
with a black outfit. Show the
world you're here, you're alive
and you're really spectacular.

You need to imagine the end
result of your weight loss
before you can actually
achieve it.

Spend some time seeing
yourself as the person you
really want to be.

Imagine a magic mirror —
when you look into it, it
reflects back everything that is
good and beautiful about
yourself.

Look in this mirror now –

in fact look every day,

at least three times

a day.

Keep your magic mirror
always with you, it will keep
you going.

Think of yourself as a chrysalis
waiting to shed its coat – soon
you will be that butterfly.

Shoot for the moon with what
you want to achieve – even if
you miss, you'll still end up
among the stars.

Success in anything you do
isn't a one-off event.
Success is a journey, not just a
destination – so enjoy the
ride.

Some days I'm more willing
to work for my dream of
the ideal me than others.

A slim future belongs to those
who believe in the beauty of
their dream. Close your eyes
and see the dream that's you
in all its true beauty.

Motivation is everything.

Willpower is nothing.

Motivation doesn't come from
willpower, it comes from
having a clear and compelling
vision of what you want.

Visualize yourself as the new
you, living your life to the full.
Repeat the exercise regularly
– this exercise works.

Use all your senses. See, hear
and feel the new you, the real
you, in all kinds of situations.

See what can be, not just what
is or has been.

The future with the new you
will be the most exciting time
of your life. And you are in the
driving seat.

Leave the past behind – you
can't change it. Live for the
dream that is your future.

You are perfectly imperfect –

which makes you just perfect.

ABOUT SLIMMING WORLD

A warm welcome awaits you at
Slimming World. Our
nationwide classes offer support
from those who have truly been
there and understand.

Our famous Food Optimising
system provides plenty to eat
and guides you through small,
simple, positive steps that will
make slimming easier than you
ever thought possible. And it's
highly practical to use in the
real world.

Inspiration and encouragement
are the hallmarks of our
approach. We will never
humiliate you, disclose your
weight or dictate what weight
you should be.

Slimming World is unique.

SLIMMING WORLD

Tel: 01773 521111

Website: www.slimming-world.com

PO Box 55, Alfreton,

Derbyshire

DE55 4UE